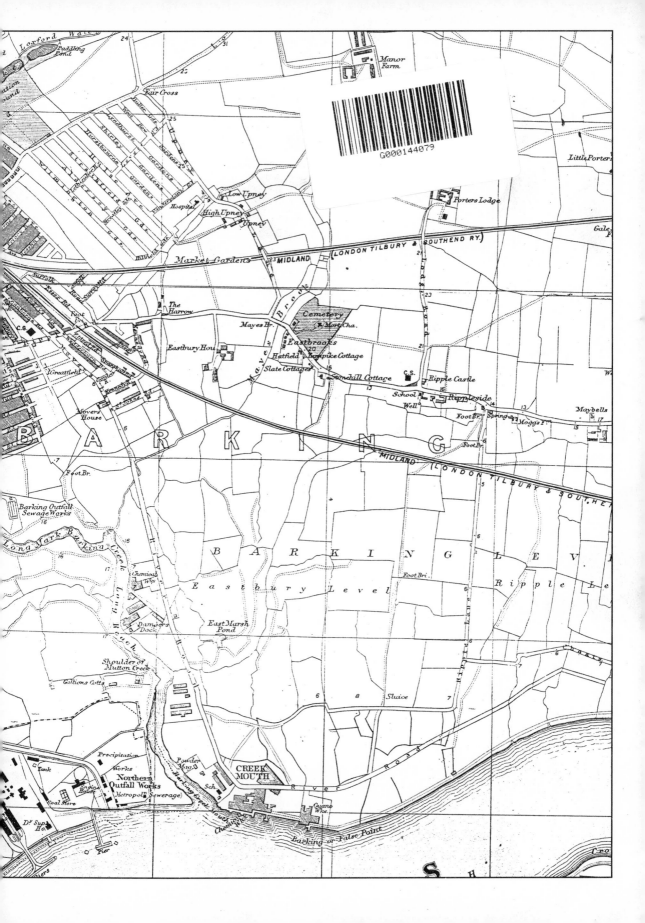

Bygone
BARKING

Barking in 1807.

Bygone
BARKING

Brian Evans

Phillimore

1991

Published by
PHILLIMORE & CO. LTD
Shopwyke Hall, Chichester, Sussex

ISBN 0 85033 795 X

Printed and bound in Great Britain by
BIDDLES LTD.,
Guildford, Surrey

To Susan, for her forbearance

List of Illustrations

Frontispiece: Barking in 1807

Acknowledgements

Many thanks to Bert Lockwood and Ian Dowling for their help and advice; also to Jim Howson for his painstaking research over the years.

Illustrations: Nos. 58-9, 75-6, 106-7, 108, 110, 156 reproduced by kind permission of the Governors of the Passmore Edwards Museum, London, E15. Nos. 7, 11, 22-3, 103, 105, 109 by kind permission of Redbridge Libraries local history collection. Nos. 37, 87b, and 149 by kind permission of Barking libraries. Nos. 39 a, b and c by kind permission of the Guildhall library.

Introduction

A Beacon for England

Old chroniclers spoke of the great religious houses as 'Beacons for England', meaning that they were places of enlightenment spreading their message afar.

Barking became a beacon of the Christian culture when its Abbey was founded in A.D.666. Barking, an early form of which is 'Berecingum', meaning 'Berica's people', was among the earliest Saxon settlements in the county. There appears to have been a high level of Saxon culture in this part of Essex, for just to the east beyond Dagenham, originally Daeccanham or 'Daecca's village', was Rainham, once *Roegingaham*, 'settlement of the ruling people'. Here a hoard of swords, spearheads, brooches, rings, shield bosses, small wooden buckets and olive green drinking horns was found.

There are indications that the Barking Abbey site may have been of religious significance long before the Saxons – in fact a beacon for pagan religion. The area was linked with other early religious centres via Green Lane, which runs through Ilford to Hornchurch, Upminster and Horndon. The suppression of these pagan centres of worship explains the rather unpromising location for a Christian abbey in the midst of a flood plain.

Unpromising or not, we can follow human habitation back before the Romans, and to the distant eras when the original users of the stone-age hand axes and flint implements, which have been found at Barking creek, Ripple Road and Gale Street, roamed these wastes. Nearby lay another site of human occupation which has revealed records of man's early progress. This is the Uphall camp location (now over the border in Redbridge). This has been shown to be a univallate fort of the Middle Iron Age, originally an enclosure of 48 acres within the angle of the river Roding and the Loxford Water Stream, and the remains of a palisade, drainage gullies, small pits, boundary ditches, marks of several round houses or storage buildings, granaries and traces of smithying – have all been found. Later a Roman military watch tower or signal station was built on the same site.

The Flowering of the Abbey

The original site of Barking Abbey was a very cramped area of land between the Roding and the Back river, 'a narrow place liable to floods'.

According to the chronicler Bede:

> This man [Erkenwald] before he was made Bishop had founded two famous monasteries, this one for himself in the province of Surrey, by the river Thames at a place called *Ceortesei* [Chertsey] ... that for his sister in the province of the East Saxons at a place called *Berecingum* wherein she might be a mother and nurse of devout women.

This happened in A.D. 666. Many endowments were made to the new foundation by Christian East Saxon princes. Much land and property was given, and the boundaries of its estate have survived until today as the area occupied by the Boroughs of Barking and Dagenham and the old Ilford borough. It is believed that the abbey was destroyed in 870 by the Danes, who in their usual fashion burned it to the ground.

Before this St Adhelm, the first English Latin scholar of note, dedicated his work *De Landitus Virginitatis* to Barking's abbess, Hildelitha, about 700. Thus it was already recognised as a centre of learning and fulfilled the role of the later universities.

Several abbesses of the Royal blood succeeded Hildelitha and Bede claims that 'many miracles were wrought here in this church at the shrines of these holy hand maidens of God', these ladies being duly canonised.

After the Danes had been cleared from Essex in the early 10th century, there is a record of property bequeathed to the reborn abbey in the year 951.

The first foundation had been a double monastery of monks and nuns under one abbess – a usual arrangement at the time. The monks and nuns led separate lives – worshipping at different hours in the church and occupying different parts of the foundation. The reforms of 300 years later by Archbishop Dunstan made Barking a strict Benedictine nunnery – the greatest in England and the only Saxon monastic foundation to survive until the Dissolution.

William the Conqueror made use of the accommodation at Barking after his coronation at Westminster Abbey on Christmas Day 1066, moving his headquarters to the town while the Tower of London was built on the site of former Roman and Saxon forts.

The abbess of Barking had precedence over all other abbesses. She ranked as a baron and enjoyed all the rights pertaining to a feudal lord, including supplying men-at-arms for the king's service when required. This often meant, however, that because the office of abbess was in the king's gift, he was apt to appoint his wife or daughter as abbess when a vacancy appeared. Maud, Queen of Henry I, was abbess for a number of years before her death in 1118, and her niece, also Queen Maud or Mathilda, wife of Stephen, was abbess until 1136. Henry II appointed yet another Maud, his daughter, as abbess in 1175 after the death of Mary Becket, sister of the Canterbury martyr, whom he had been persuaded to appoint two years before she died.

After King John's surrender to the Pope in 1213 changes occurred, and the principle was eventually re-established that the nuns should elect their own ruler who was then (often tardily) given the royal seal of approval.

The abbess had the support of a considerable number of officials, including principally the prioress, elected for life to manage the business affairs of the abbey and also standing in for or complementing the role of the abbess in services. There were two sub-prioresses, a cellaress and under-cellaress (who supervised and purchased stores for the abbey's catering and other needs), a nun kitchener, a yeoman cook and a pudding wife – these were elected or re-elected annually. The chantress saw to the running of church services and rehearsed the singing. The sacrist was responsible for the church cleaning and decoration for special days. The almoner and the firmaress tended and consoled the poor.

In 1381 John of Gaunt paid over £50 to the abbey for the *novitiate* fees of an Elizabeth Chaucer – believed to be the poet Geoffrey Chaucer's daughter, as Gaunt had been a patron of Chaucer in other ways.

So it can be seen that, although the abbey had remained as in its origins an aristocratic institution, it widened its intake to a certain extent during the last two centuries of its existence to include the daughters of wealthy commercial families. Isabel de Basinges, abbess from 1291-4, for instance, was a member of the family whose London house gave its name to Basing Lane (now Cannon Street). Many Essex families such as the Tyrells of Little Warley and the Fitzlewes of West Horndon sent their daughters to the abbey.

The last abbess, Dorothy Barley, was from a noted Hertfordshire family and fulfilled her difficult role with honour and dignity.

The Last of the Abbey

In 1536 came the first wave of suppression of the great religious houses. Somehow Barking escaped, although its annual income of £1,080 gross was well above the limit set to avoid dissolution. The nuns were probably aware that it was only a matter of time and luckily, as usual, they had a supporter in a vital role. This was Dr. William Petre, the up and coming lawyer from Devonshire, prospering in the king's service. He had become a personal friend of Dorothy Barley, the last abbess, and his own sister-in-law was a resident nun. As King's Commissioner he received the deed of surrender from the hands of the abbess on 14 November 1539 and ensured that within a fortnight the nuns were given pensions according to their seniority.

During the two years of demolition we learn a tremendous amount about the nature of the building through the accounts of James Needham, Surveyor-General to Henry VIII. An extract, which attempts to give some flavour of the original, follows:

> From Sunday XIX daie of June to Sunday XVII of July (33rd Year of Henry VIII) Payments made and payd for Our Souveraigne Lord the King for work done by his Grace's Comaundement in undermynding and casting downe the late Abbey Chyrche of the King's manor of Barking for the providing of the fayrest coyne stones and others to be ymployed of the King's mansion of Dartforde; as well as upon wages to artificers and labourers, clarke and others; and also empcions of stuff bowght requescted for the said work wt. land carriage of stone, as the pticular payments thereof payd by the hande of my Mr. James Nedam his said Grace's Survear-Genall more playnly doth appear; that is to wit, Sondaye the XVII daye of Julye exclusive by the space of a moneth.
>
> *Carpenters*; Working not onely in taking down and breking uppe the bordes of the cloyster wt. other tymber and not only working but also making the handbarowes and whele barowes and in like maner helmyng of pyckaxes and other necesares for the myners and labourers to occupie.
>
> *Myners*; working not onelye undermyndinge and casting downe of Rownde Towres but also taking uppe the benches in the cloyster and in lyke man^r. providing of the fayrest coynestones and other coyne stone for the loding of lighters to be ymployed at the Kinges mansion at Dartforde.
>
> *Comyn Labourers*; working not onelye in ridding and clering owte the ffayrest and best coynestone, casting the rubbyshe a syde and not their working oneleye but also the land carriage of the said stone from the late abbey to the water syde.
>
> *Empcions*; To Richard Wodland a smyth for making of VI new pycaxes of his owne iron. For land carriage of stone at XVld by the day from the late Abbey of Barking unto the water syde where the creeke cometh oute of Teimes to Barking.
>
> *The Clerke*; Gevyng attendance in overseign the mynars and laborers and not soe onelye but keping the checke booke of the same.

Needham's account follows the same pattern month after month, ending on 10 December 1542. In August 1541, carpenters are engaged in 'taking down the timber in the steple' while miners are 'undermyndinge the steple and other places of the late abbey chyrche'.

Barking Abbey: materials used:

Early: Stone from Caen, Barnack, Binstead.

Later: Reigate stone and, during the pre-dissolution period, some brick.

Site: 11 acres.

Estate: 57 acres, brought £7 15s. 4d. in 1540, included Convent Mead, a pasture called 'Huntyng', a decayed barn, 'a bushe pasture ground', an enclosed vineyard, 'well set with elmes and well stored with coneys', a keeper's lodge, Grange Meadow, the Grove 'at West end of the late Abbey with orchard and garden'. Fishponds on north-west, fed by river.

Outward Bound: The Fisher Port

The origins of Barking as a port arise from the convenience of its 'pool', where the Thames comes inland to meet the Roding. Early man may have travelled up the creek from the Thames and found this haven where the Roding meets the creek. The Saxons found this whole area made a good centre and a group of villages came into being. As well as Barking there was a prosperous community stretching through Dagenham, Rainham and Mucking, as revealed by archaeological finds. Contact between these villages is likely to have been water-borne, as the land routes may often have been flooded and impassable in the Dark Ages. A fishery is mentioned at Barking in 1086 but this was probably confined to the river, whose water then was pure. However, an early mention of salt-water fishing by men from the town occurs in 1320 when there was a law case in which the City of London, as conservators of the Thames, prosecuted local fishermen for using nets with too fine a mesh. This seems to have been a recurring problem, for in 1406 the *Liber Albus* of the city records a further dispute. Apparently there was almost a riot in the Roding and adjoining fishing localities when the size of the meshing on the nets was again challenged. The nets were seized by Alexander Bonner, a sub-conservator, and taken to Barking, where a mob of fishermen and their friends rescued them from the custody of a constable. Fortunately, after several fishermen from 'Erehite, Prattys Ferye, Berking and Wulwiche' were taken to Westminster and found guilty, wise counsels prevailed, and they were allowed to fish with the existing nets until the next Easter when they had to provide new nets according to the 'Standard of London'. Thus ended a dispute which could have set the Thames on fire with insurrection.

In the days of Barking Abbey the abbess exercised her own control over fishing and levied a small toll known as 'herring-silver' on the catch.

Many Barking men were volunteers or were coerced into the Navy during times of continental conflict, where their skills, no doubt, were much appreciated.

In the reign of Charles II the Dutch Navy gained such ascendancy over the British that they blockaded the Thames and burned British ships in pursuance of trade dominance at sea. One of the defence measures hurriedly decided upon was the sinking of ships in Barking creek, according to the diarist Samuel Pepys. A few years before, Pepys had ventured out to Waltham Forest and Ilford in order to see the timber used for the King's ships, and its method of measurement. This timber was carried by whim to Barking where there was a slide into the creek. There the wood was made up into rafts, and was floated on the Roding and Thames to the Woolwich and Deptford dockyards.

In the 19th century Barking became one of the greatest of British fishing ports. There were several reasons for this: apart from its convenient location there was also the matter of the 12 ft. difference between high and low tide which made the careening or heeling of boats for repair a simpler task.

The Hewett family, whose 'Short Blue Fleet' increased the economic prosperity of Barking, was very active until the decline in the 1860s caused by the railway reaching east-coast ports, the non-adoption of sharing the catch as part of the wages, and the disaster of December 1863, when 60 men died in a gale off the Dutch coast. The industry and Hewett's fleet relocated to Lowestoft and the east coast, but repair work on the fishing smacks was continued until 1899.

Several contemporary commentators have left us a vivid picture of the fishing aspect of the port. W. Glenny described the purlieus of Heath Street in the halcyon days:

In the older part of town near the wharf where fishing smacks were careened for the purpose of cleansing, calking and repairing – a place redolent with tar and the odour of ships stores; abounding with nets, new and old, with rope-walks for spinning hawsers and twine; where might be purchased waterproof coats, leggings, sou'westers and big boots ...

Thomas Auckland recalled:

I was never so much in my element as when at Barking among the fishermen and smacks. The pretty vessels ... are as fresh in my memory as when they were afloat and I recall the Barking days of my youth as the happiest of my life. How fragrant Heath Street and Fisher Street smelt, of tar and pitch, how well the stores were supplied with oilskins, guernseys, red caps, hawsers, ropes and twine. How the boys marched about the town at fair-time, and enjoyed the fun, as if there never were gales or high seas off the Doggerbank and the coast of Iceland.

W. Glenny concluded that:

There were two seasons when every fisherman liked to be ashore; the one occasion was Barking Fair, on October 21 or 22, the other was ... Christmas. Gingerbread shows [displays of gingerbread made into the shapes of people and animals], dancing and drinking were the attractions of the former festival, whilst good cheer and family meetings distinguished the latter.

The Fields of Youth

Jeremy Bentham (1748-1822), the philosopher and legal reformer knew and loved the fields and riverside of Barking in his boyhood. As he was a sickly baby, born in London, it was decided that the fresh air of Barking where his father had a country seat would be good for him, so his childhood was interspersed with long periods of residence with his paternal grandmother in Heath Street. He delighted in gathering great bunches of wild flowers from the local fields. Looking back in old age he also remembered the flowers in the garden of the house:

So long as I retained my [sense of] smell, a wallflower was a memento of Barking, and brought youth to my mind; for the wallflower covered the walls, with their roots between the bricks.

In the early years of the 19th century Elizabeth Fry used to take her children to the family's holiday cottage by a wild and sandy spit of land at Dagenham beach. A daughter, Louisa, recalled the journey from the London end of Essex, which was still rural even when she had grown up and married. Two verses of one of her poems are as follows:

> Onward we went, the sun appearing,
> Painted with faint light the meadows nigh
> When Barking's fair Monastic archway
> And grey old Church we can descry.
>
> And then appeared the *Ship and Shovel*
> And little Wayside Turnpike too.
> With thriving farms so well remembered
> Until 'The Chequers' came in view.

By 1874 Louisa's sister, Katherine, wrote that, compared with their early memories, 'This rural country is now greatly spoiled ...'.

A local chronicler, J. Frogley, writing 70 years ago, described the *Ship and Shovel* inn as a modern building of red brick and a well-known house:

In the past all kinds of sports were held here, especially pigeon shooting matches. Side of the house is a lane leading to the marshes and Horseshoe Corner ... a safe place for grazing cattle. The keys of [the gates of] the marshes were kept by the landlord of this house and singularly his name was Samuel Keys.

The licence of the *Ship and Shovel* dated back at least to 1740. The marshes behind it, being very isolated, were used for many an unlawful venture. In the 1830s some Barking men were involved in a smuggling incident in which a cargo of tobacco was landed here. The Revenue had, however, got wind of the attempt and, as the contraband was being carried across the marshes, seized both men and carts. The men were sentenced to prison for 12 months. Another event requiring seclusion was a fight between two pugilists, Parrish and Hadbrook, on 12 March 1820. After 41 rounds Parrish emerged the victor, without apparently the illegal encounter being interrupted by the authorities – so the choice of location proved remote enough.

In *A Tour Round England* (1870), Walter Thornbury mentions the local working children tending the 'great tracts of potatoes that bloomed around Barking', destined for the London market. Other writers describe the long walls of manure surrounding the cottages preparatory to spreading on the fields.

Mr. H. Wand noted that Barking in 1890 was a very compact little town:

Although some development had taken place east of the railway, that side of town still remained almost wholly under agriculture. Rippleside was a straggling village stretching from the Cemetery to the 'Chequers', and isolated farms and groups of cottages were to be seen along Ripple Road, these being mainly occupied by farm workers. Ripple Road was quite narrow then, bounded on each side by high banks and hedges and overhanging elms. Traffic on the roads beyond the developed area was mainly restricted to the farms, and heavy wagons, laden with market garden produce left the farms in the evening, and, after a long pause at one of the public houses en route, ambled off to Stratford or Spitalfields.

Even by 1963, Barking had not quite lost its capacity for rural surprise. In that year, when an Essex farmer was adopted as a Tory Parliamentary candidate for Barking, he little expected to find nestling among the large industrial concerns in the district – a working farm. The story, reported in a national newspaper, mentioned that this latter-day rural phenomenon in Jenkin's Lane, Barking, was overshadowed by a huge paint factory and run by the three Attreed brothers, whose family had been farmers for more than 100 years.

A Beacon for England

1. The granting by King Sebbi of the East Saxons of a Charter, which confirmed land and privileges to the newly instituted Barking Abbey in A.D.666. Ethelburga, approved as abbess, kneels next to her brother Erkenwald, Abbot of Chertsey. The illustration was drawn by Foster Jarrett.

2. An eighth-century copy of 'Hodilred's Charter'. This confirms the grant of lands to the new abbey by Œdelraed, kinsman of Sebbi, c.687. The document is written in Latin uncial script on parchment, with creases which indicate a long period of folded storage. The abbey was already accumulating fame and benefactors as its influence spread, and its buildings began to fill the original cramped site between the Roding and the Back river.

Carta Hodilredi, patris Sebbi Regis Eaſt-Saxonum, Terras Abbatiſſae Monaſterii de Beddanhaam (modo Berking) concedentis.

Ex Autographo in libro Bibliothecae Cottonianae, dicto Auguſtus II, N.º 26, reſervato.

INNOMINE DÑI XPI SALUATORIS Quotiens scīs ac uenerabilib. locis uestris Aliquid offerre uid tur Uestra uobis reddim ur on nostra largit qua propter ego hodilredus parens sebbi proui a east sexanorum Cum ips us consensu propria u lu tate Sana men te in eroq: consilio Tibi hedilb urg eabbatissae Ad aug men tum monasterii tui quae dicitur beddanhaam perp tualiter trado et deo eo ire in tuo trans scribo teri am Quae appella tur ric ng baam budinbaam decenbaam angenlabesbaam Etcappo insilua quae dicitur uid mundes felt Quae simul sunt coniuncta X L manent uotusqadterminos quae eum pertinent Cum omnib. adse pertinentib. Cum campis siluis pratis et maris co Ut tam tu quam posteri tui teneatis possid extis Et quaecumq: uolueris deeadem facere terra liberam habeatis potestatem Actum mense martio ettestes conpetenti numero ut subscriberent rogaui Siquis contra hanc donationis kartulam uenire temp tauerit aut corrumpere Anteom nipoten tem dm et ihm xpm filium eius et spm scm Id est inseparabilem trinitatem Sciatse condemnatum et separatum ab omni societate xpian Q kartulam donationis in sua nihil om nus firmitate etut firma etin concussum sit donuc ter mini sunt autem isti huius faerre cuius quib: accin cit ab oriente fritola burna abaquilone centinces triub et hanc dem stede abau strale fluomen tam isa Siquis autem hanc donationem augere uolue rit augeat os bona sua in regione uiuorum cuis scis suis sine fine amen

†Ego sebbi rex east sax pro confirm ontione subscripsi Ego oedel raedul do ator subscrpsi
†Ego erknuual dus epis copus consensi et sub scripsi Ego uul fridus epc con sens et sub
†Ego uaed de epis con sn et sb Ego cuda pr et abbas consenti ens subso
†Ego egc baldus pr et ab con sen et sub sp

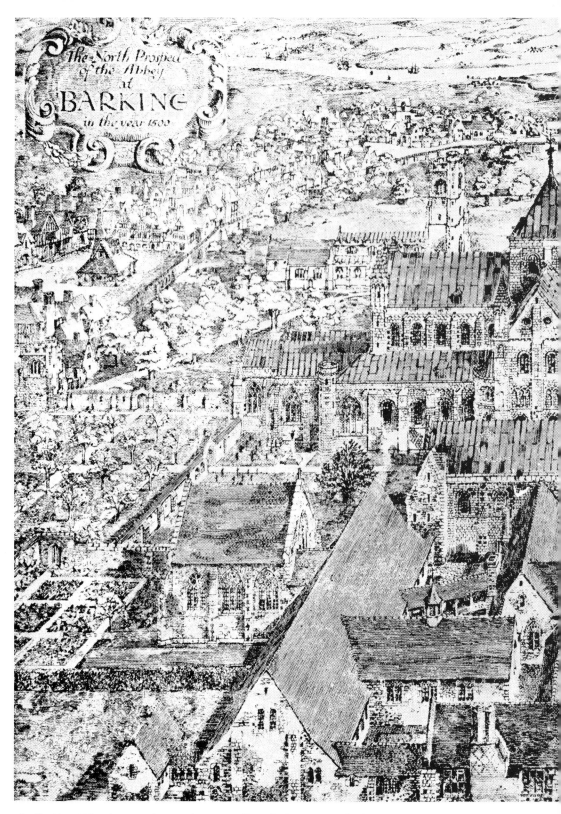

The North Prospect
of the Abbey
at
BARKING
in the year 1500

3.   Barking Abbey became the most important Benedictine nunnery in the country. Its impressive stature both architecturally and in terms of ecclesiastical and political power are mirrored in this reconstruction by Sir Charles Nicholson, which shows the abbey at its peak towards the end of the Middle Ages. The main abbey building was cruciform and about 338 ft. long – into this church the nuns processed eight times on ordinary days, and more on feast days, in order to sing the daily sequence of offices.

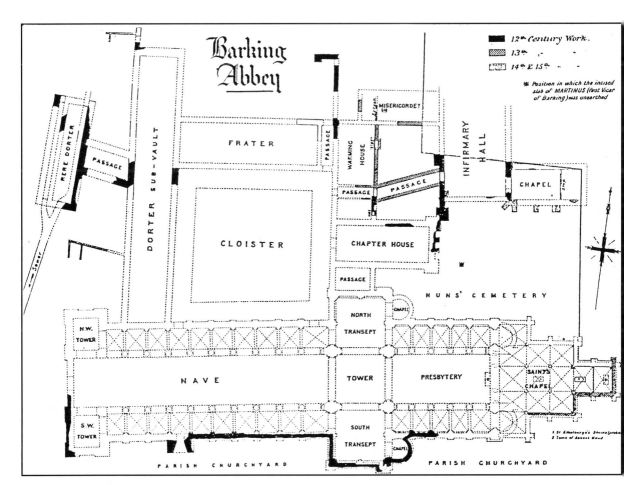

Barking Abbey

12ᵗʰ Century Work.
13ᵗʰ ·
14ᵗʰ & 15ᵗʰ ·

✳ Position in which the incised slab of MARTINUS (first Vicar of Barking) was unearthed

RERE DORTER

DORTER SUB-VAULT

PASSAGE

Sewer

FRATER

PASSAGE

WARMING HOUSE

MISERICORDE?

PASSAGE

PASSAGE

INFIRMARY HALL

CHAPEL

CLOISTER

PASSAGE

CHAPTER HOUSE

NUNS' CEMETERY

PASSAGE

CHAPEL

N.W. TOWER

NORTH TRANSEPT

TOWER

PRESBYTERY

SAINT'S CHAPEL

NAVE

S.W. TOWER

SOUTH TRANSEPT

CHAPEL

1 St. Ethelburga's Shrine (probab
2 Tomb of Abbess Maud

PARISH CHURCHYARD

PARISH CHURCHYARD

4. Clapham's plan of the abbey following the 1911 archaeological investigation. The chapter house, in the middle, saw formal meetings of nuns and abbess. The long building across the cloister contained on the first floor the dorter, or dormitory, with its stairs leading down into the abbey church for the nuns' night devotions. Underneath, the 166 ft. long building held offices and storage for the cellaress who had to buy enormous quantities of food and wine, not only for the nuns, but for visitors and the resident staff, including the priests who celebrated mass.

5. A fragmentary portion of the shaft of a Saxon cross found built into the churchyard wall. The four sides are decorated with typically elaborate and well preserved knot-work. Very few of the many Saxon crosses which once existed have survived, and this one is a relic of the earliest abbey.

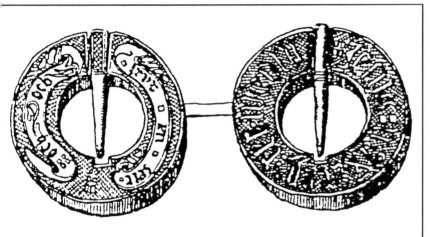

6. An ancient *fibula* or brooch found in the ruins of Barking Abbey. Nearby, a gold ring came to light, on which was engraved the Salutation of the Virgin, and the letters J. M.

7. The stone rood of the 12th or early 13th century in the upper floor of the Curfew Tower, the only remaining building from the abbey. It was originally a gateway, one of a number leading to and from the precincts. Pevsner points out the similarity of this rood, formerly in the Chapel of the Holy Rood, to the figures also in relief which survive at Chichester.

8. A view of the abbey remains in the 1920s. In the background of this shot (on the left) is the impressive elevation of the Church of England National school which from 1872 carried forward the torch of learning which was handed down the centuries by the abbey community. At the rear right-hand side is the Curfew (or Firebell) Gate, and to the left of this a chimney represents the secular commercial and industrial town.

Outward Bound: The Fishing Port

9.   This watery view of the quay with fishing smacks and fishermen dates from 1831. One can almost hear the sound of voices echoing across the pool. At this time there were about 120 smacks sailing in pursuit of North Sea catches and even some further afield. In mostly locally built boats they were supplying the demands of London's rapidly growing population.

10. The men who manned the boats were a hardy crew. In addition each vessel in 1864 carried four apprentices who were bound to the trade for seven years.

11. Here we see a Barking smack fishing for cod off the Dogger Bank. A smaller boat is hauling up the lines. This is dangerous work in the breaking swell, as the small boat is half filled with water to keep the fish alive. The fish are thrown into the boat as the lines are hauled in, while the smack tries to act as a breakwater by keeping to windward of the smaller vessel.

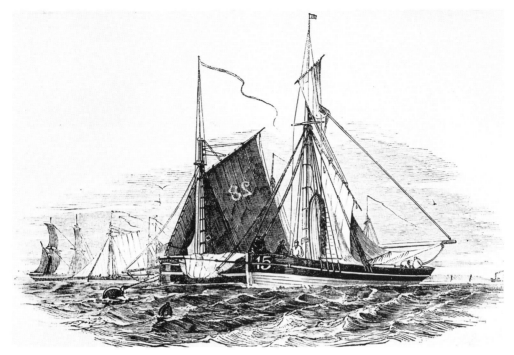

12. Barking fishing smacks, *c*.1860. They were described by Thomas Auckland as 'pretty vessels' with names such as *Ranger, Racer, Leander, Ocean Pacific, Blue Bell, Tartar, Saucy Lass* and *Transit*. At the conclusion of the trawl the hard work of winching the rope and net on board is undertaken. An old writer has described the scene, as the fish tumble out, thus: 'what a motley crowd there is, too! Besides the flat fish and cod, there is hake, haddock, whiting, ling, and a few stray herring. Slimy, wriggling, goggle-eyed skate; long curling conger eels; fish of all shapes and sizes, jumping flapping and floundering about on the wet, slippery deck'.

13. A fast carrier-cutter has hoisted her flag to take in fish cargoes for market. Rowing boats from the fishing fleet swarm round the cutter like bees, each trying to deliver boxes and hampers of fish. Sometimes the cutter has to make sail and force its passage to avoid being swamped. The hands on board would stow up to 40 tons of fish (500-1,000 packages and 18 tons of ice) in the holds as fast as they could.

14. Down by the Thames was the hamlet of Creeksmouth and this inn, the *Crooked Billet*, provided shelter in a rather desolate spot.

15. Barking creek facilitated the fishing trade and other seaborne commerce. It may have also provided access to marauders from across the North Sea, such as those who are thought to have attacked and destroyed the earliest Barking Abbey.

16. The *Princess Alice*, a pleasure steamer, was on its way back to London from the trippers' resort of Rosherville Gardens, Gravesend, when it was rammed by the *Bywell Castle*, an iron collier, on 3 September 1878, between Barking and Woolwich. About 650 men, women and children perished in a few minutes, the filthy state of the river water probably making the disaster worse. Many sad souvenirs in the form of plates, handkerchiefs and commemorative paper items were produced, shortly after the tragedy.

17. The Thames could be a hazardous place with the very busy waterborne traffic of the 19th century. The steamer *Batavier* was one casualty off Barking in 1872. A salvage operation is underway. Two children were drowned on 19 October when the Rotterdam-bound cargo and passenger boat collided with a Turkish man-of-war trying out her new engines along Barking Reach.

18. A view of the pool, framed by boats of various kinds. Quite a stack of timber is laid out on Page Calnan's Wharf and on board the barge on the left. The buildings on the quayside are obviously flourishing in this Edwardian picture.

19. *S.S. Empress* (of London) at work in the pool. Note the working dress of these Edwardians, including rolled up shirt-sleeves and caps.

20. The Town Quay. The loaded barge on the right sits very low in the water, while on the left-hand barge the hatches are off. A crowd of mostly male onlookers, some probably unemployed, watch operations – perhaps in the hope of picking up a small job.

21.   A view of the Town Quay 20 years later. More modern vessels lie at anchor in the pool and J. John Masters' Abbey Match Works can be seen beyond the quay towards the right.

22. These old buildings on the Town Quay in 1925 await demolition.

23. A close-up before demolition of the shop which supplied the Barking fishing smacks from *c*.1800 to *c*.1845-50.

The Last of the Abbey

24. The last abbess and her nuns take leave of the abbey in 1539 after handing over the Deed of Surrender and the keys of the premises to the king's commissioner. The picture was drawn by Foster Jarrett.

25. The abbey seal, 1539. At the top is the crowned virgin; below, St Erkenwald between St Ethelburga and St Hildelitha; at the bottom an abbess.

6. Plan by Smart Lethieullier dated 1722, showing part of the abbey site with two remaining gates. The curfew gate, nearest the church which had contained the Chapel of the Holy Rood, is on the left. The North gate (taken down in 1881) is on the right, about 350 ft. further on.

7. The North gate had been reduced to a simple arch by the time this print was published in 1821. Originally the upper storey, seen in Lethieullier's plan, had contained the Chapel of St Nicholas, referred to in the 1456 abbey rental. A third entrance to the precinct, known as the Great Gate, was apparently near the Town Quay, where the abbess had 'two paier of staires' allowing access to the river.

28.   View of the Curfew or Firebell Gate at the end of the 18th century. The name explains the secular use as a bell tower, which had ensured its survival. Its convenient central position near the market also helped the gate's new career.

29. St Margaret's parish church seen through the churchyard trees earlier this century. At first it was probably only a chapel, which was made into a parish church by the intervention of Abbess Anne de Vere about 1300. It was still within the Abbey precincts, however, and therefore was partially controlled by the Abbess. In 1254 the rectory of Barking was held by the abbey authorities and there were two vicarages called 'Northstrete' and 'Southstrete'.

30. The parish church interior in the 1920s. In the 14th century each of two vicarages of Barking were held by a separate individual. The 'southern' vicar officiated at the abbey church and the 'northern' vicar presided at the parish church, his income supposedly coming from the northern part of the then very large parish of Barking, which is now mostly part of Ilford.

31. John and Elizabeth Tedcastell from their memorial brass in the church. Elizabeth died aged 43 in October 1596. Spaces on the brass were left blank, to be filled when John eventually died (28 March 1612). John was one of the younger Brethren of Trinity House, a Freeman of London and a member of the Merchant Taylors' Company. He married a second time, but directed in his will that 'I John Tedcastell ... sick in body: to be buried and laide by my first wife Elizabeth, in the parish church ... if it be not too costlie the carryinge and buryinge there'.

32. These naive drawings of two of the sepulchral monuments in St Margaret's are typical of early 19th-century representations.

SIR CHARLES MONTAGUE, KNT.

CAPT. JOHN BENNETT.

33. In 1849 this niche was discovered in the wall of St Margaret's. R. Windle, a local artist, recorded it.

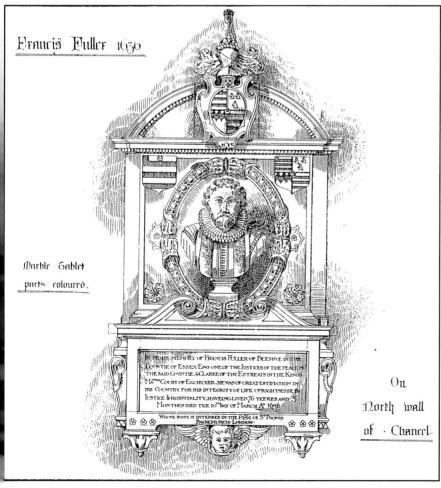

Francis Fuller 1636

Marble Tablet
parts colourd.

On
North wall
of · Chancel

34. The fine marble tablet to the memory of Francis Fuller, 1636, which gives details of the important offices he had occupied during his career.

35. The new King Edward VII appointed a second suffragan bishop in the diocese of St Albans, with the title of Bishop of Barking, 362 years after the abbey was surrendered. The Venerable Thomas Stevens, Archdeacon of Essex was nominated and consecrated on 17 February 1901, at St Margaret's, Westminster. The Bishop used postcards with a drawing of the last seal of the Abbey printed on them to keep in touch with his clergy.

36. This postcard of 1908 shows the Bishop residing at the Vicarage, 'close to Barking station' (card to the Rev. Mr. Wright of Sandon). The vicarage at present lies neglected behind the new Vicarage Field shopping mall.

Old Seal of Barking Abbey.

FROM THE BISHOP OF BARKING.

Trains from Fenchurch Street, or District Stations, less frequent from Liverpool Street, or St. Pancras.

Telegraphic Address Bishop, Vicarage, Barking.

House close to Barking Station.

By all means. I will be the Relishan In will be absent. Hope you may have a good change and find weather if you like to Weymouth. J Barking

Kindly excuse Card. Ap. 21. 1908

The Fields of Youth

7.   An idyllic scene at the Wellington Mill, in 1895,
ustrated by Bennett Bomford. This stood on the
mer marshland, south of London Road, and was
nstructed in the year of Waterloo, hence the name.

38.   A strange early 19th-century print showing
a scene near Barking, with rustic cottages and a
view along a creek into the Thames.

39. Three houses of note at the end of the 18th century.
a) Bifrons in 1794.

b) Fulkes (the Vicarage House) was on the east side of North Street, on the northern corner of the former Nelson Street. It was occupied as a vicarage for a time before the present vicarage was built in 1794.

c) Westbury Hall.

40 a & b. Two of the famous names who roamed the fields and riverside of Barking, and testified to its rural charms. The philosopher Jeremy Bentham, whose fully clothed skeleton, with a facial likeness created in wax, still sits in a glass box at University College London, lyricised on his childhood in the village.

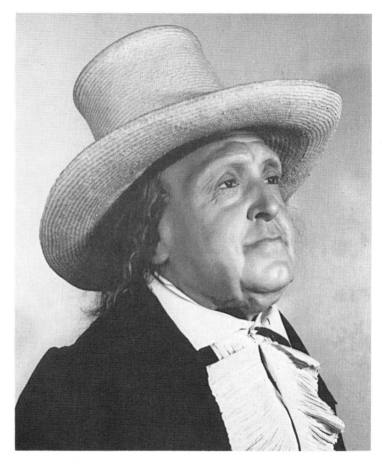

Elizabeth Fry, the great prison reformer, was a member of the Barking Quaker Fellowship.

41. Thatch and timber farm buildings at Barking remind us of the numerous farms that once dotted the map.

42. Cottages at one of the bends in Longbridge Road. The farthest cottage appears to be offering refreshment to the holiday traveller on foot or bicycle.

43. Rippleside in former days was a quiet hamlet strung out eastwards along the edge of the marsh. The dusty road led past primitive cottages. By the time this photograph was taken, in the early 20th century, the land in the distance had been developed as a cemetery. A chapel rises above the fields.

44. The way to Goodmayes in the 1900s is neatly signposted next to a boundary stone and a small obelisk. The spectators appear to have time on their hands while the photographer records the quiet scene in Longbridge Road.

45. The folly-like Ripple Castle. How the Edwardians loved to enjoy the country lanes, for this house has also been adapted for the supply of refreshment, judging by the ginger beer advertisement at the gate.

46. To the west of Barking, beyond the hamlet of Wallend, in the 19th century. The road towards London led to the village of East Ham, where the thirsty could rest awhile within the quaint walls of the *Old White Horse*.

47. A gaslit end of Upney Lane. The labourers'
cottages of plain sober brick seem sturdily built and
contrast with the high Edwardian dress of the two
ladies in the background.

48. High summer in Upney Lane before World
War One, and two walkers encounter a horse-
drawn haycart.

49.   Another haycart passes into the distance as it rounds a stationary delivery van. This photograph dates from *c*.1906.

50. Looking back along the same bend shown in the previous photograph at about the same date. The ladies are having a serious discussion, unaware that they are being photographed for posterity. At the back of the fence is the ubiquitous refreshment garden.

51. A shady Water Lane, c.1905.

52. A late Edwardian autumn in Gale Street. The lodge sits in the middle of a veritable spinney of trees. Several branches have been lopped from the tree on the far right, presumably to stop them falling in windy seasons. The dress of the man standing in the road suggests a job in the City, but may only be Sunday best.

53. The beginning of the end of the country, c.1920. Although Longbridge Road has an improved surface and pavements have been constructed alongside, the urban effect is slightly moderated by the small flock of sheep approaching in the background.

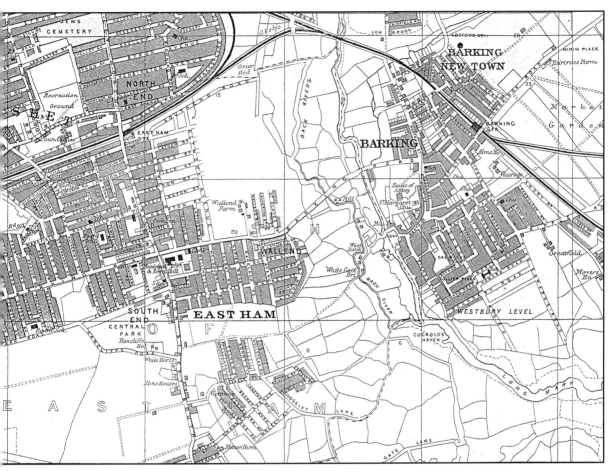

54.   In this plan of 1905 Barking town still has open land around its perimeter. On the north-east is Faircross Farm, and below that are market gardens. To the south, Westbury Level reaches out to the Thames and Barking creek. To the north-west an osier bed is marked out near the railway lines to East Ham. Wallend Farm is to the north of the hamlet of that name. The northern outfall sewer runs across the bottom left corner down towards Beckton, and above that is Manor Farm.

A Goodly Place for Commerce

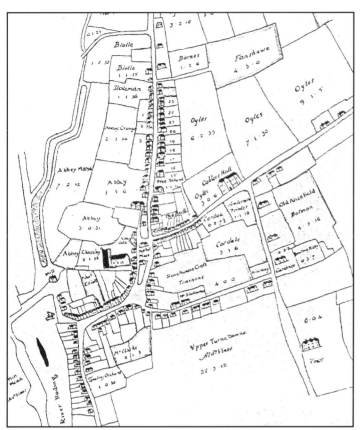

55. Barking in 1653. In 1086 the manor of Barking had one of the highest populations in Essex (*c*.250 people), and by 1670 there were 461 houses in the whole parish. In 1653 the town centred around the church, market place, mill and quay. The Curfew Gate and *Bull Inn* premises are marked. Dovehouse Croft, north of the present Axe Street, recalls the days when pigeons were kept as an extra source of meat.

56. The Leet House was erected in 1567 and took exactly one year to build. Detailed accounts of the works are in the Bodleian Library, Oxford: the total cost is shown as £324 9s. 10d., and this was borne by Queen Elizabeth so that the building 'should serve as Her Majesty's Courte and for a Towne House and Market House for the benefitte of the Inhabitants'. R. N. Whiston's reconstruction of the Leet House, known as the 'Old Town Hall' in later times, shows its two-storied timber-framed construction. The Market Hall section on the ground floor was entered through four open arches, the timber posts of which stood on Kentish ragstone bases.

57.   The early shops clustered around the Market Hall had disappeared by the 19th century. On the left in this picture, *c.*1903, is the *Barge Aground* in the Broadway. Robert Willett's glover's and hosier's shop is on the right of the picture. Willett owned a number of retail shops in the town including a pawnbroker's.

58. The Market House was becoming rather dilapidated by the 20th century.

59. The upper room viewed from the north-east corner in its latter days, when it was used for meetings by the Vestry and other official bodies. The original staircase of solid oak was situated at the west end with an entrance from a doorway at the front of the building. This led to the Court House upstairs, where justice was administered in a hall that extended the length of the building. Later this was sub-divided by a partition at the south end, and the walls were enclosed with deal panelling, seven ft. high.

60. Royal coat of arms in plaster, with the date 1588, from the Leet House.

61. Eastbury House in 1783. Chance ensured that this house, among the many manor houses and mansions that made Barking a rich man's retreat, would survive. Clement Sysley, a wealthy merchant of East Ham, bought the Eastbury estate and soon after, in the late 1550s, built the present house. During the 18th and early 19th centuries, when the estate ownership was divided, Eastbury was lived in by a succession of tenant farmers. The house became very dilapidated, and in the 1830s it was about to be pulled down. Edward Sage, an antiquary, championed its retention because of its architectural and historical heritage.

62. A ground plan, showing the division into rooms and offices. Building development began to threaten the house again in earnest in 1913-14, when parts of the estate were sold for housing. A white knight in the shape of the Society for the Protection of Ancient Buildings appeared and raised money. The London Survey Committee of the London County Council was also available to research and publish a monograph on the house, raising its profile, and during the 1920s the building was bought by the National Trust.

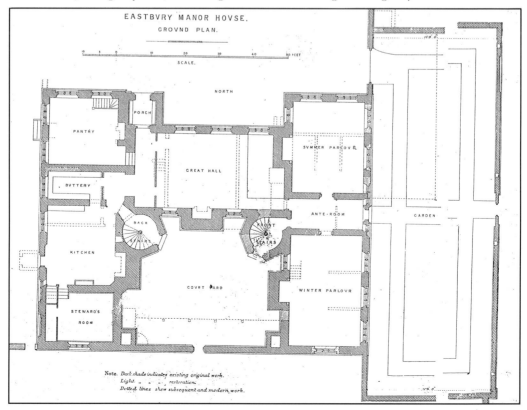

63. An early 19th-century view of Barking, emphasising its rural charm.

64. James Cook probably saw a town like that in the previous illustration when he came back to Barking after a campaign with General Wolfe in America, to marry a local girl at St Margaret's. It was 21 December 1762 when Cook, with £291 in his pocket, earnings from surveying the St Lawrence River, married Elizabeth Batts, she being 21 and he thirty-five. John Constable explained this mystery by claiming that James had stood sponsor to Elizabeth at Barking many years before, when he was only 18, and had said: 'If this infant lives I will marry her'.

65. More Barking water – this time by the Wellington Mill. When this was built in 1805 there was a growing demand for flour, a demand stimulated by the rapidly rising population, the Industrial Revolution, and Napoleon's shipping blockade, which affected supplies from the Continent. Many new mills were built in Essex, and substantial houses and premises to go with them. With the shipping of vast quantities of American grain, however, local mills were in the doldrums again by the early 20th century.

66.   A view down the short street that led from the Broadway to the Curfew Tower and the middle of Back Lane, in 1909. On the Broadway corner is a second shop belonging to Robert Willett, dealing in clothes. At the back is the entrance to Young's auctioneers (upstairs), with an advert for 'Half houses to let'. Willett's announces 'Beckton shirts at 2s. 6d.' – presumably these are for heavy work use, by those locals employed at Beckton's Gas Works and other factories.

67. A 'B' type omnibus of the General company (B974) roars up a busy Broadway in 1913. In the middle of the picture is the *Bull Inn*. The No. 23 bus route was typical of the services now linking Central London with areas out of town. These were made possible by the greater reliability of the new 'B' class vehicles which stood rather high off the ground and ran on solid tyres.

68. At Loxford triangle, on the border with Ilford, a shopping parade, seen here *c.*1908, provided a selection of services, including a general grocery store, newsagent and tobacconist, hat shop and dining rooms.

69. A sign of late Victorian and Edwardian commercial growth was the spread of shops from the High Street into more residential thoroughfares. This view of Gascoigne Road in the 1920s shows the result.

70. The coming of the gramophone and wireless sets created a demand for shops which sold records and other items, as these record sleeves show. Albons Stores, with shops in both Ripple and Longbridge Roads, also sold cycles, whereas Symphonie Salons specialised in music and theatre tickets.

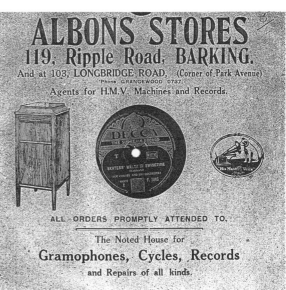

The End of Innocence

71. The massive works for the construction of the northern outfall sewer (Beckton), in May 1864. The wooden ladders and rigs seem out of place on such a project, but steam power is in use on the railway and elsewhere on the site.

72. The new London sewage outfall system created in the Victorian era relied partly on gravity and partly on pumping stations, like this one at Stratford.

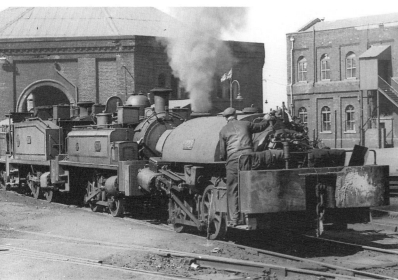

73. Engines and wagons at Beckton gas works in the 1950s. In the background the distinctive architecture of the original retort houses can be seen, giving some idea of the massive scale of this enterprise, which lay partly in Barking, down by the Thames. They were opened in 1870 to supply a large area of East London, but Barking itself had its own town gas-works for many years. Gas was not supplied from Beckton until after 1912. Many of the workers at Beckton, however, came from Barking.

74.   Hewett's Yard, Barking Creek. Although Hewett's 'Short Blue' fishing fleet migrated to Lowestoft and other east coast ports in 1854, according to Benham, or in 1865, according to the Victoria County History, smacks still returned to Barking to refit until the end of the century. Before this the yard had built many of the vessels in the fleet. In its last Barking years the 'Short Blue' fleet consisted of 152 trawlers and 46 'longliners'.

75.   The aftermath of the 1899 explosion at Hewett's Yard, showing how near to houses the works were on the landward side. This event effectively put an end to the refitting work and finally severed the fishing boat connection.

76. A 1948 advertisement for J. John Masters' Match Works features an aerial view of the town, in which many details of its layout can be made out. These include the light-coloured block of the Capitol Cinema and Marks and Spencer's near the top left margin.

WHERE MASTERS'

MATCHES

ARE MADE

AERIAL VIEW OF

ABBEY

MATCH WORKS

BARKING

J. JOHN MASTERS & CO. LTD.

HADDON HOUSE, 66a FENCHURCH STREET, LONDON, E.C. 3

77. Two of the matchbox labels issued by J. John Masters, avidly collected by schoolboys in the post-war period when less sophisticated amusements were in vogue. Earlier versions gave their address as Barking rather than London.

78. This interesting early commercial vehicle – No.6 in the fleet belonging to the Michelin Tyre Company in the 1920s carries the name of their Barking works on its side. Note the motoring coats, protecting the driver and his assistant from exposure to the elements when aboard the moving vehicle.

79. In its early days Barking station, opened in 1854, was rather a primitive affair, half hidden down a side street. H. D. Welch says, however, that in contrast the line was extremely efficiently run. The management was farsighted and had a 'policy of cheap fares and matchless punctuality'.

80. Looking across the level crossing to the station *c*.1900. The London, Tilbury and Southend Railway had originally been planned to carry Londoners to Tilbury riverside; from there they could be ferried across the Thames to the famous pleasure gardens at Rosherville near Gravesend. Freight traffic was also expected on a large scale, in the form of imports from Thames Haven. These original objectives were forgotten when Southend's rapid rise made it the new resort that holidaymakers, including those from Barking, could enjoy at low cost.

81. Looking across the station level crossing in each direction. The *Railway Hotel* was extremely convenient for the passenger

82. Engines on the L.T.S.R. were lovingly looked after by their crews, and locomotives were often named after places along the line. Here is 'Barking', with the railway company's coat of arms on its side, *c*.1908. It had been built by Sharp Stewart in 1880.

83. In 1912 the London and Tilbury was taken over and absorbed into the Midland Railway. No. 2104 still carries the little name-plate on its front. The destination reads Southend as the operating staff pose proudly.

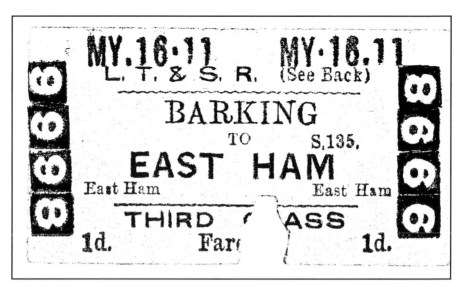

84. On 16 May 1911 a passenger travelled from Barking to East Ham on this One Penny, Third Class ticket. It is fascinating to speculate on the reason for the trip, whether for work, shopping, visiting a relative or going to a funeral – public transport was used so widely for every purpose in this era. More intriguing is how the ticket came to be preserved 80 years later as good as new.

85. Goods wagons for use by John Byford, c.1905. The writing reads across the wagon. Byford had premises in London Road, Barking, and was a merchant for lime, cement and similar materials.

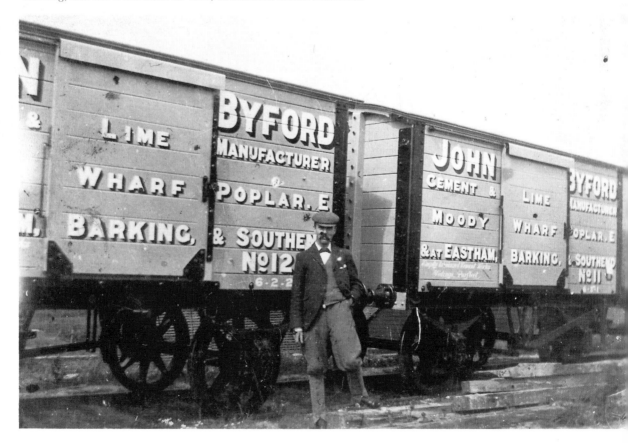

86. Improvements to the L.T.S.R. line were being made all the time. New stations were opened at Upton Park in 1877 and West Ham in 1901, while Barking station was rebuilt in 1889 and again in 1905-8. This latter rebuilding involved widening the section between East Ham and Barking: extra land had to be acquired, the layout of the station was altered, the level crossing was closed and a new bridge was provided to carry East Street over the railway and station. When the new station was complete, electric working by District trains was extended to Barking, from 1 April 1908.

On the Edge of the Abyss

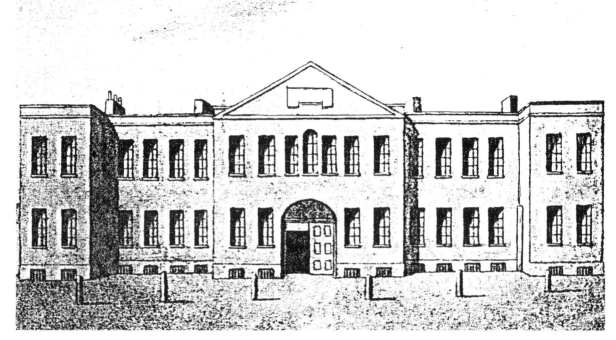

87 a & b. The Barking Workhouse, North Street: an early drawing, and a later wash drawing by Bennett Bamford showing the shops that were built on to it by 1905. A limited amount is known about life in the workhouse. It began as four tenements leased in 1721 from a man known as Blackburn Poulton. Later part of the new workhouse was used as a school, and this school survived until the 19th century, long after the new Union system created a central workhouse for a large number of parishes, including Barking, at Oldchurch, Romford.

88. James Cumberland becomes a chimney sweeper's apprentice: 'This indenture made the 15th day of April in the 7th year of the Reign of our Sovereign William the Fourth ... 1837. Between William Glenny and Richard Evans, Churchwardens of the Parish of Barking in the County of Essex and Samuel Milton and William Baker, Overseers of the Poor of the said Parish of the one Part and John Martin in the Parish of Barking ... Chimney Sweeper of the other Part'.

89. '... have put, bound, and by these presents do put and bind James Cumberland a poor boy of the said Parish of Barking, being the age of 10 years to be apprenticed to the said John Martin to learn the Trade, Business, Art and Mystery of a Chimney Sweeper, and with him to dwell remain and serve from the Day of these Presents for and during the Term of 6 Years ...'. After no doubt seeing the inside of many a chimney, James eventually became his own master in Romford, and is buried in the old cemetery, Main Road.

90. A page from the Barking Select Vestry Minutes, 30 January 1830. Winter was very hard for the poor, sick or out of work Barking resident in the last century. The first entry states: 'Relieved 38 families, 38 Single Persons with 195 four pound loaves at 7 pence and 170 lbs of Pork at 4 pence a pound'. By the next week there was a rise to 54 families and 61 single people!

91. The cemetery was a familiar place to many families in the 19th century. The journey down Ripple Road often ended with the interment of the latest infant or child of the house. Malnutrition and unhealthy living conditions conspired with poverty to aid the grim reaper. This view was taken in the early 1900s.

92. Ripple Road. By Edwardian times, the general standard of living had risen a little. Although there were many more people in Barking, cheek by jowl in unsuitable and often unhygienic housing, there were more industries, more shops and more services to give employment. Many of these were extremely labour-intensive. Even so, Barking applicants for the forces at the start of the First World War were often, like those elsewhere, found to be in poor physical shape.

93. Ripple Road by the *Harrow*. Street works are in progress and seven labourers are at work. Various horse carts filled with wicker baskets and wooden crates are stationed about the street. Not a plastic item in site, nor a mechanical digger – only picks and spades are seen in this view, *c*.1913.

94. East Street in the 1920s, with Blake's Corner a familiar building. This was a furnisher's and ironmonger's business owned by a Councillor Arthur Blake and constructed about 1911-12. The better furniture in such a shop was just a dream to the poorer resident. His or her 'bits' would be handed down from deceased relatives or would be acquired from the secondhand shop.

PUBLISHING OFFICE OF
The
BARKING ADVERTISER
FAULKNER'S
NOSEGAY
SHAG
97
CLARKE
DAM
COLLAPSE
540
DROWNED
DEATH
35.

95.   East Street, west of Blake's Corner, *c*.1912.

96.   Looking towards the Broadway from East Street Post Office, *c*.1913. A person's carefully husbanded sum put away into Post Office savings might provide enough to buy a secondhand table or washstand in the shop next door, where the goods are stacked up and lashed to the front. By 1914 trams were running from the Broadway at the bottom end through to Aldgate via Poplar and Limehouse. The trams in East Street run to Chadwell Heath, Goodmayes and Ilford.

97.   The *Bull* corner at the bottom end of East Street, at the Broadway Junction, before the trams arrived in 1905. Cyclists are recommended to the accommodation at the *Bull*. Several men and boys seem to have time on their hands. The *Bull* is in fact numbered as 2 North Street, round the corner.

98.   Further round the bend, more shops down to the *George* are revealed, together with the *Barge Aground* on the far side of the market, and beyond that Edwin Burn, clothiers. This photograph was taken *c*.1904, before the era of tram-tracks.

99. Left from the end of East Street *c.*1913, the curve of the Broadway is revealed, veering off to the bottom end of town and towards Heath Street and the Town Quay. William G. King is a 'working draper and milliner' according to his shopblinds. Yet another of Willett's emporiums is seen just this side of the Congregational church. Pelling's Stores at 11 sells groceries and a second store further on at 21 deals in oils and colours, a description now defunct.

100. A front view of E. Burn's shop. The date on the side pillar is 1902. Before moving to this new shop Alfred Edwin Burn had traded from 5 Heath Street, a less central location.

101. In the early 1900s a motley collection of buildings lines the end of the Broadway. The *George Hotel* has been rebuilt in a florid late Victorian manner. The lamp standard nearest the camera, known as the 'three lamps', was a place for public meetings of workers, as it was on the way to and from work for employees of the factories and works by the river.

102. Heath Street, leading to the Quay and
Fisher Street *c.*1907. This contained the Branch
Headquarters of the National Union of Gas
Workers and General Labourers, as it became,
in the Coffee Tavern run by a Mr. Smythes who
was Branch Secretary. In 1889 a subscription
was organised at the Tavern when the men's
organiser, Bill Watkinson, a worker at Beckton,
lost his job. The money raised – £13 – enabled
him to open a shop, also in Heath Street, selling
newspapers, tobacco and radical tracts.

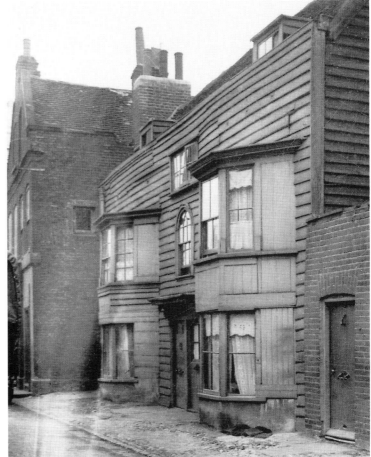

103. The old wooden houses in the short street
leading to the Fire Bell or Curfew Tower, which
is behind the photographer to the right. Back
Lane runs to the left and right behind the
camera. The scene was photographed *c.*1930.

104. Only the Curfew Tower survives from this crowded scene, looking the other way from the previous photograph. No less than 24 children, mostly dressed in their best clothes, pose for the camera, suggesting a Sunday, *c*.1904. The old house on the left offers good beds for men at only 6d. per night.

105. Exchanging gossip in Back Lane in the 1920s, shortly before the houses were demolished. Even in this quiet backwater a motor vehicle has made its appearance.

106. Close-up shot of houses on the east side of Back Lane, *c.*1929.

107. View from the churchyard of houses in Back Lane, before their demolition in 1933.

108.   This photograph of the west front of the Court or Leet House in Back Lane during the 1920s could be mistaken for a David Lean recreation of a Dickensian episode. The grittiness of daily life in Barking's back streets at this time is immediately conveyed.

109. Tucked away off Axe Street and awaiting demolition in 1933 are these very old cottages. The top of the *George Hotel* is seen over the rooftops. These lanes were built on the site of the former Bifrons House.

110. The same row of buildings about 1930. The small structure in the centre of the picture was a candlemaker's *c.*1870. The contrast between old and new is provided by the cinema posters.

111. Before the extension of London Road in 1936, westward-bound traffic had to negotiate the bend in North Street. Today all is superseded by the new rotary system, leaving no time for a quiet conversation or window-shopping. Notice, on this photograph of *c*.1913, the tram stop on the left, placed incredibly close to the corner.

112.   The same corner, looking in the other direction *c.*1910. Priggen's corner shop was not only a newsagent, stationer, confectioner and tobacconist but also sold games and toys. Next door is Pallot's, another little shop, and then Steers', which mysteriously advertises 'famous seasoned hearts'. A little further on is the ubiquitous Willett's store – this one a furniture dealer. Finally, it is a surprise to see the old Barking Workhouse block still surviving.

113. By the *Royal Oak* in Longbridge Road, two carters have pulled into the kerb to slake their thirst. Carting was a heavy job as it involved much loading and unloading. Driving needed vigilance to spot the unexpected hazard, even on the uncrowded highway of Edwardian times. For instance, one might meet an early car – an alarming prospect for a horse and driver.

BARKING.

PLACES OF WORSHIP—Abbey Church, St. Margaret's: vicar, the Rev. A. Bloomfield; curate, Rev. Robert Russell; officiating minister, Rev. John Reginald Corbett; organist and choir master, Mr. Fred T. Dawson; clerk, D. J. Watkins. —Congregational Church, Broadway : minister, Rev. J. Smedmore—Baptist Chapel, Queen's-road—Wesleyan Chapel, East-street : minister, Rev. James Palmer—Primitive Methodist Chapel, Manor-road : minister, Mr. G. H. Fowler—Plymouth Brethren, Cross Tree : various ministers—Roman Catholic Church, Linton-road: priest, Rev. J. Gilligan.

SCHOOLS—National, North-street: master and mistress, Mr. King and Mrs. Fisher ; infant, Miss Waters—Independent—Roman Catholic: mistress, Miss Wayman.

VESTRY—Clerk, Mr. William Blewitt.

BENEFIT SOCIETIES—Barking and South Essex Perpetual Benefit Building Society: secretary, Mr. James Linsdell ; meetings held at the Town Hall second Monday in each month—A Court of Foresters, No. 2,339, is held at the George Inn second and fourth Monday in each month, 398 members ; secretary, Thomas Forge—Provident Brother's Society, held at the Ship Inn first Monday in each month.—Provident Benefit Society, held at the Town Hall, established upwards of 40 years ; meeting nights, the first Monday in the month.

CARRIERS—To London: John Jaggers and Charles Leftley.

GAS WORKS are situate in Hart-street—A company was established in 1839, issuing 300 £5 shares, which were sold to Messrs. Hulett and Co. in 1858, and a new company was formed in 1867 to supply Barking and Dagenham, capital £20,000 in £10 shares; price of gas per 1,000 feet, 6s; secretary, Mr. J. T. Cazaly; manager of works, Mr. William Barnett; collector, Mr. James Linsdell.

INNS—Blue Anchor, J. Millard ; Britannia, Thomas Lewis; Bull, G. Parsons; Crooked Billet, Henry Coates, Creek's Mouth; George, J. Holmes; Peto Arms, J. Bailey; Queen's Head, Robt. Bowler; Red Lion, Susan Bosworth; Rose and Crown, Louisa Milton; Ship, H. Linsdell; Ship and Shovel, S. Keeys; Still, Frederick Henry Clarke; Fishing Smack, Henry Seabrooke; Spotted Dog, E. Maynard.

LITERARY INSTITUTIONS—The Mutual Improvement Society gives entertainments and concerts during the winter months. Has a library at the Town Hall ; librarian, Mr. R. D. Wilding; hon. sec., Mr. J. Bissell—Church Library, Town Hall.

PHYSICIANS AND SURGEONS—Messrs. Parsons and Mac Donald, Mr. R. F. Scott and Dr. Mc Manus.

POST MASTER—Mr. H. Stephens.

REGISTRAR OF BIRTHS, DEATHS AND MARRIAGES, AND SANITARY INSPECTOR for the District of Barking Town and Ripple Ward, Mr. R. D. Wilding.

SAVINGS' BANK—At the Town Hall; open every Tuesday evening; actuary, Mr. C. Mumford.

THE POLICE FORCE consists of two sergeants and twenty constables, including mounted patrol and one constable stationed at Creek's Mouth; station, North-street.

THE TOWN HALL is over the Market-house, and is used for courts leet, public lectures, &c. It was erected in the reign of Queen Elizabeth.

114. *The Essex Annual*, 1872. A succinct summary of the main institutions of the town. Note the benefit societies – a source of help and an encouragement to thrift to those who could manage the subscription. One of the carriers by road is Charles Leftley, of the famous family firm whose vehicles feature in this book.

115. The Salvation Army Citadel in Ripple Road, between the Park Coffee Tavern and terraced houses. Like the other denominations it helped to provide community care and companionship for those in need, which is still in demand today, but which was a blessing in the 1890s and 1900s.

116. A moment of disaster in the mid-1930s. Barking Salvation Army Hall on fire, as caught by a passing local photographer

117. The Salvation Army Band *c*.1907, making a joyful sound in hard times.

118. A garden party of railway workers and friends at the 'Manor' in 1907.

119.   Where these Edwardian grannies are going in a Leftley's wagon is an intriguing puzzle. From the flags it appears to be a celebratory outing or carnival. This picture is a striking reminder of how people aged much more quickly before health education and proper dental care. Low wages and long hours of drudgery meant that many people were worn out at a comparatively young age.

120.   Barking crippled children's outing at Loughton, in September 1912. Kind benefactors at Loughton invited parties of disabled youngsters from different areas to enjoy a special day in the country.

A Walk in the Park

121. Going to the Park in 1911. The 76 acres were opened in April 1898 and soon became popular. The lodge house, next to the gates in Longbridge Road, is one of the smartest to be seen in a municipal open space.

122. Parks were immaculately groomed in the earlier decades of this century. Local councils and people were inordinately proud of their environment, and interference from central government was minimal. In this scene, c.1907, a horse-mower operates in the background while a watchful 'parky' is ready to pounce on dropped litter and deal with unruly behaviour.

123. A summer's day in the park, *c.*1908.

124. A surprisingly elaborate vessel was imported to give an interesting trip around the lake in the 1950s.

125. The promenade behind the boat house in 1906.

126.   A relaxed scene at the boat house. This photograph was taken before 1914.

127. Pushing the boat out at Barking Park, 1917. Some young Barking sailors are learning the art of sail, but too late to join the fishing fleet.

128. The fine bandstand, seen here in 1929 and now demolished, was an attractive feature of the park.

129.   Racing to see the balloon lift off from the 'Rec.' at Carnival time, 29 July 1907.

130. A decorated boat on the lake, part of the carnival celebrations in 1907.

131. A splendid float with a Roman theme made the 1908 Carnival well worth watching.

Out of Struggle, Progress

132 a. Schedule of Fares and Stages (April 1933). Ilford Council ran the Broadway to Barkingside route for many years. At Ilford it joined the Chadwell Heath service.

SCHEDULE OF

FARES AND STAGES

	WHEN WORKING:—	
BARKING BROADWAY AND KHARTOUM ROAD BARKING STATION AND HAMPTON ROAD LOXFORD BRIDGE AND ILFORD BROADWAY HAMPTON ROAD AND CONNAUGHT ROAD ILFORD BROADWAY & SEVEN KINGS STATION CONNAUGHT ROAD AND BARLEY LANE SEVEN KINGS STATION AND GROVE ROAD SEVEN KINGS HOTEL AND CHADWELL HEATH ILFORD BROADWAY AND PERTH ROAD HAINAULT STREET AND HORNS TAVERN PERTH ROAD AND BARKINGSIDE	HAMPTON ROAD AND BELL INN	**1**D.
BARKING BROADWAY AND HAMPTON ROAD BARKING STATION AND ILFORD BROADWAY LOXFORD BRIDGE AND CONNAUGHT ROAD HAMPTON ROAD AND SEVEN KINGS STATION ILFORD BROADWAY AND BARLEY LANE CONNAUGHT ROAD AND GROVE ROAD SEVEN KINGS STATION AND CHADWELL HEATH ILFORD BROADWAY AND HORNS TAVERN HAINAULT STREET AND PRINCES ROAD BELL INN AND BARKINGSIDE	LOXFORD BRIDGE AND BELL INN HAMPTON ROAD AND PERTH ROAD	**1**½D.
BARKING BROADWAY AND ILFORD BROADWAY BARKING STATION AND CONNAUGHT ROAD LOXFORD BRIDGE AND SEVEN KINGS STATION HAMPTON ROAD AND BARLEY LANE ILFORD BROADWAY AND GROVE ROAD CONNAUGHT ROAD AND CHADWELL HEATH ILFORD BROADWAY AND BARKINGSIDE	BARKING STATION AND BELL INN LOXFORD BRIDGE AND PERTH ROAD HAMPTON ROAD & HORNS TAVERN	**2**D.
BARKING BROADWAY AND CONNAUGHT ROAD BARKING STATION AND SEVEN KINGS STATION LOXFORD BRIDGE AND BARLEY LANE HAMPTON ROAD AND GROVE ROAD ILFORD BROADWAY AND CHADWELL HEATH	BARKING BROADWAY AND BELL INN BARKING STATION AND PERTH ROAD LOXFORD BRIDGE AND HORNS TAVERN HAMPTON ROAD AND BARKINGSIDE	**2**½D.
BARKING BROADWAY AND SEVEN KINGS STATION BARKING STATION AND BARLEY LANE LOXFORD BRIDGE AND GROVE ROAD HAMPTON ROAD AND CHADWELL HEATH	BARKING BROADWAY & HORNS TAVERN LOXFORD BRIDGE AND BARKINGSIDE	**3**D.
BARKING BROADWAY AND BARLEY LANE BARKING STATION AND GROVE ROAD LOXFORD BRIDGE AND CHADWELL HEATH	BARKING STATION AND BARKINGSIDE	**3**½D.
BARKING BROADWAY AND CHADWELL HEATH	BARKING BROADWAY & BARKINGSIDE	**4**D.

WORKPEOPLE'S RETURN TICKETS are issued up to 7 a.m. for MALES and 8 a.m. for FEMALES at the following Fares:—

FOR ANY 1d. ORDINARY FARE AT 1d. RETURN.   FOR ANY 3d. ORDINARY FARE AT 3d. RETURN.
   „   2d.   „   2d.   „   4d.   „   4d.

PARCELS OTHER THAN PERSONAL LUGGAGE WHICH CAN BE CARRIED ON LAP OF PASSENGER, ONE PENNY PER PARCEL OR ARTICLE AT PASSENGER'S OWN RISK.

CHILDREN IN ARMS FREE, otherwise Children up to 14 years of age at the following Fares:—

FOR ANY 1d. ORDINARY FARE ½d.   FOR ANY 2½d. OR 3d. ORDINARY FARE 1½d.
   „   1½d. or 2d. ORDINARY FARE 1d.   „   3½d. or 4d.   „   2d.

TRAMWAYS OFFICES,
LEY STREET, ILFORD.

L. E. HARVEY, A.M.I.E.E., M.Inst.T.,
Manager and Engineer.

b. From 31 May 1914, Barking withdrew from a joint agreement to run trams to Aldgate from Loxford Bridge that had been in operation for a couple of years. From this date a Barking Broadway to Aldgate service was run jointly by trams from East Ham, West Ham and the London County Council. (Extract from L.C.C. list, 1932.)

67 BARKING BROADWAY—ALDGATE   S 5½d   R 9. 46 *Mins.*

Via Barking Rd., East India Dock **WEEKDAYS**   **SUNDAY**

From	Rd., Commercial Rd. E.	FIRST	LAST	Sats.	FIRST	LAST
BARKING	to Aldgate	4 58, 5 12	11 35	11 35	7 54	11 50
	to Blackwall Tunnel ..	4 58, 5 12	12 12	12 18	7 54	12 5
ALDGATE	to Barking	5 1	11 35	11 32	7 14	11 29
„	to East Ham Town Hall	5 1	12 15	12 12	7 14	12 13
„	to Blackwall Tunnel ..	5 1	12 15	12 12, 1 50	7 14	12 32

FIRST to Aldgate from East Ham Town Hall 4 50
     from Green St. 4 37, from Canning Tn. 4 35
„ Blackwall Tunnel to Barking 4 45, 4 56, 5 8
Sats. LAST Blackwall Tunnel to Aldgate 1 30

First E. Ham Town
Hall to Aldgate 6 40
Last E Ham T. H. to
Blackwall Tnl. 12 22

133. Barking open-top car No. 4 on the Barking station approach section of East Street in 1907. This was operating the Loxford Bridge to Fisher Street service, a short route which ran for only three years.

134.   An open-top tram on the bridge over the rebuilt station, *c*.1912.

135.   Tram No. 7 lies forlornly on its side in Jenkin's Lane, on the far shore of the Roding, after overturning in a gale on 27 December 1913.

136.   The Bascule bridge was built specifically to take the Beckton Tramway across the Roding. Because the river was used by sailing craft berthing at the Town Quay, a novel opening mechanism designed on the rolling cantilever principle was adopted. There were three spans: the northern or Barking section contained an over-head gantry (24 ft. long) on which stood the control cabin. The bascule or centre span is being raised here by two 33 h.p. motors, *c*.1911.

137. A 1920s view of the bridge, which could be lifted in three minutes. To dispense with overhead wires, an arrangement of side contacts was used which touched the lowered skate fitted to the cars. It was not until repairs in 1917 that it was discovered that cars could coast over the section using their own momentum.

138. Tram No. 336 on route 67, passing the *Victoria Tavern* on its way to Barking in the latter days of tram operation, before trolleybuses took over.

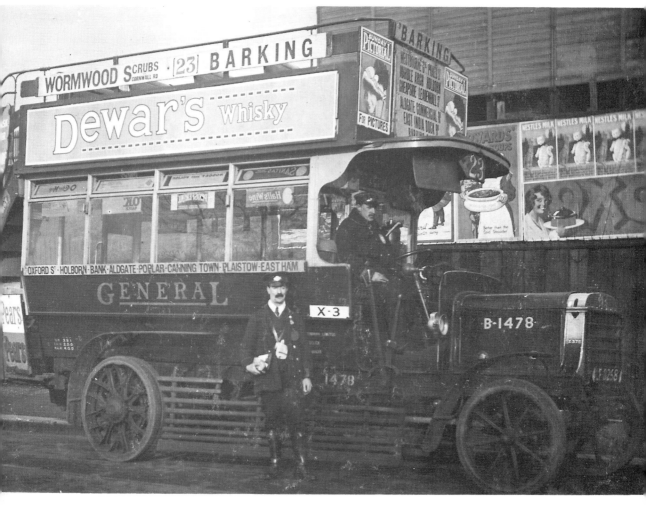

139. A solid-tyred B1478 on Route 23 (Wormwood Scrubs Cornwall Road to Barking) in the early 1920s.

140. Martin, an independent operator, bought this Dennis four-ton bus on 30 July 1927, and ran it on Route 151 (Barking station to Becontree).

141. Buses to and from Rainham and London throng the centre of Barking near Blake's Corner at the beginning of the 1930s. The Capitol Cinema (the white building in the background on the right) can just be seen.

142. Leftley's display three different types of vehicle for the conveyance of goods of all kinds, in the late 1920s.

143. As the 20th century moved through its first three decades the town's streets took on an air of entering the mainstream of national trends. Linton Road looks very solid and respectable in this view, with its laundry, houses, shops and other institutions. The *Brewery Tap* has the characteristics of a suburban pub, such as might be found on the fringe of any town centre.

144. Rural Upney Lane has smart new pavements and is in the process of having its road surface improved to cope with modern traffic. In the late 1920s the volume of road traffic, both private and public, was increasing rapidly.

145. Longbridge Road in the 1930s is fully equipped with police box, signs to the east coast, modern shops and high-level street lighting.

146.   At the end of East Street, a single trolley wire is installed overhead, preparatory to the introduction of trolley buses on the Loxford Bridge section on 6 February 1938. The London Road route saw trolleys introduced on 8 June 1940. The rebuilt *Bull* has a 'lounge and luncheon bar' typical of the 1930s.

147. The Public Offices, East Street, c.1905, home of the Urban District Council and also of the free Public Library which held 8,500 volumes. This building had been erected by the Local Board at a cost of £12,402. The Public Baths, which were built in 1899 for £8,250 behind the offices, were used in winter time as a public hall. To the rear were the fire station, electricity works, town yard, stables and public mortuary.

148. Barking police station, Ripple Road, c.1910. A constable shows off the uniform of the period. In 1911 Inspector William Crawfourd had a staff of eight sergeants and 40 constables.

149.   Barking fire and ambulance station in the 1920s, with contrasting vehicles on parade. Motor appliances were being adopted throughout Essex during this decade. In 1925 the Chief Officer of the fire station was Captain E. J. Abbott who had a staff of 20 firemen.

150. An early view of Rippleside, showing the National school *c*.1894. A later building was constructed in 1896. In 1906 the average attendance was 160, the master was W. J. Parker and Miss A. M. Perry was in charge of infants.

151. Barking Abbey school, seen here in the 1930s, was a public secondary school, founded at Faircross in the 1920s. It perpetuated the name of the abbey and its reputation as a centre of learning after a break of hundreds of years. The headmaster was Major E. A. Loftus. Major Loftus appeared in the *Guinness Book of Records* on account of his extraordinarily long teaching career. After he retired from the Abbey school he continued to teach in Rhodesia, where he died aged over 100.

152.   A delightful photograph of Westbury school *c.*1908, Ripple Road, built in 1902. The railings are thronged with children, hardly surprising as this school could find places for 520 pupils in each of three categories – girls, boys and infants – making 1,560 in total. The average attendance was somewhat lower in 1906 – 339 boys, 400 girls and 280 infants.

Barking
Free Churc
Athletic Association
Ladies
Gymnasium
April
1919

53. More than one trend is illustrated by the Barking Free Church Athletic Association Ladies Gymnasium Group of April 1919. Women were seeking to build on the emancipation gained through taking over in wartime what were traditionally men's jobs; the churches were a centre of social activity in both the old and new parts of town; and the 1920s and '30s saw a revival of interest in athletic pursuits such as rambling, cycling and athletic movement. The Women's League of Health and Beauty promoted a gentler predecessor of today's aerobics.

154. A high point in Barking's progress: the town is given Borough status. Here the Guard of Honour formed by the 4th Battalion of the Essex Territorials is inspected by H.R.H. Prince George who salutes the colours, 5 October 1931.

155. During the official Incorporation of the Borough, H.R.H. Prince George is seen here talking to Mr. J. Drain, Barking's Victoria Cross holder, a bus driver in civvy street.

156. For Charter Week the Public Library in Ripple Road, built for £13,000 and opened in 1924, was attractively floodlit by gaslight. Forty-three years later, on 4 April 1967, an arsonist set light to the building and in minutes 78 years of work and a collection of treasures accumulated since 1889 were destroyed.

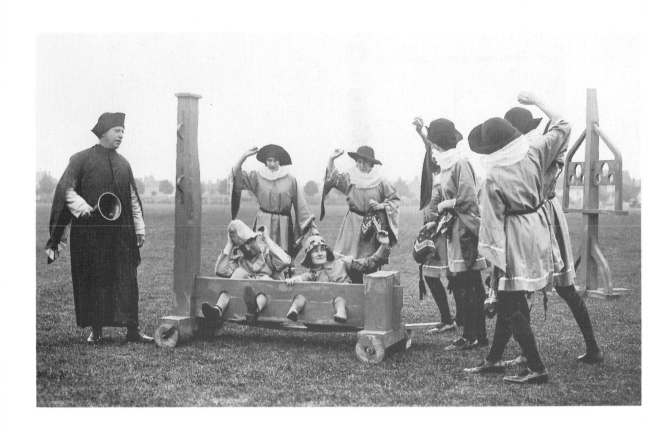

157. The Historical Pageant in Barking Park, held to celebrate the granting of Barking's borough status.

158.   The new Barking. Contrasting styles of 'Tudorbethan' in Longbridge Road emphasise the spread of suburbia in a working-class town.

159.   The torch is passed to future generations. The impressive buildings of the South-East Essex Technical College in Longbridge Road pointed the way to opportunity for many local youngsters.